Busy Beavers

Nancy Hicer

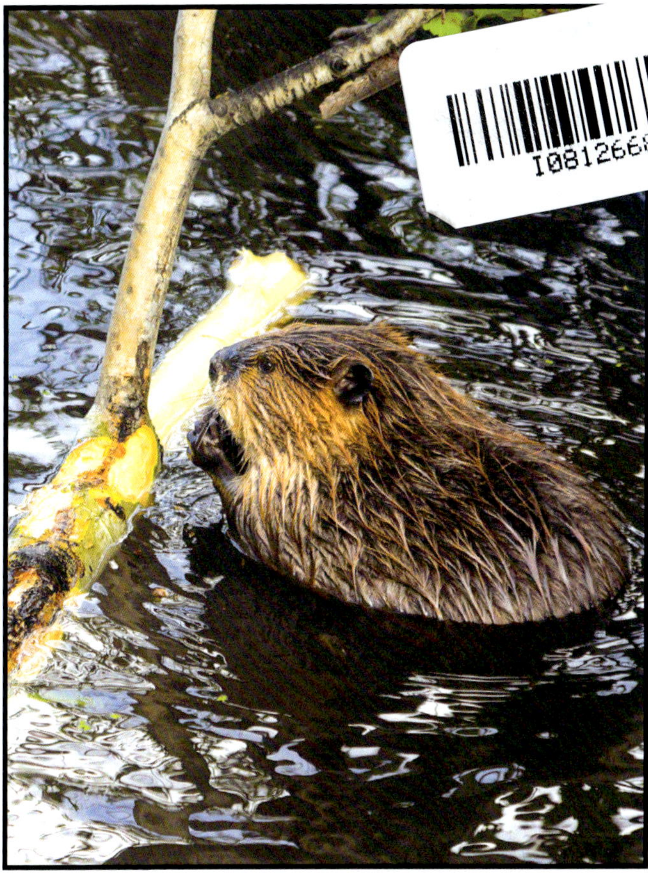

Rosen REAL READERS

Rosen Classroom™
New York

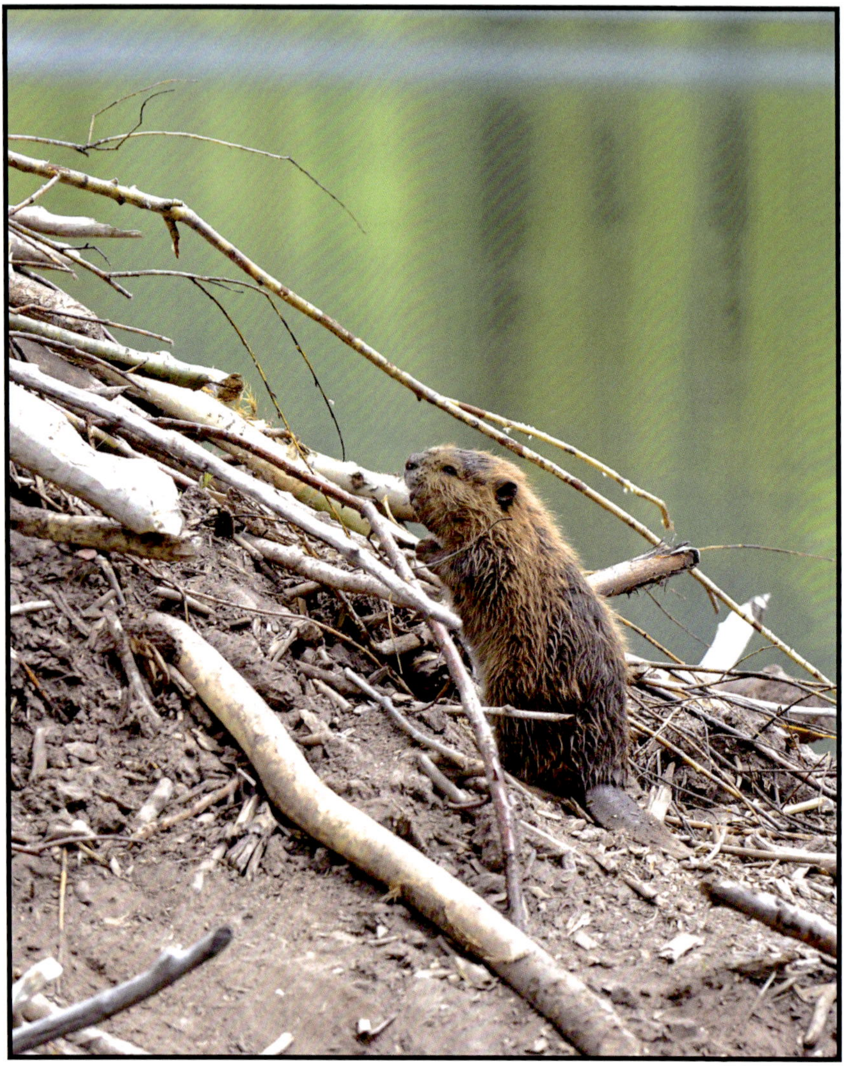

This is a beaver.

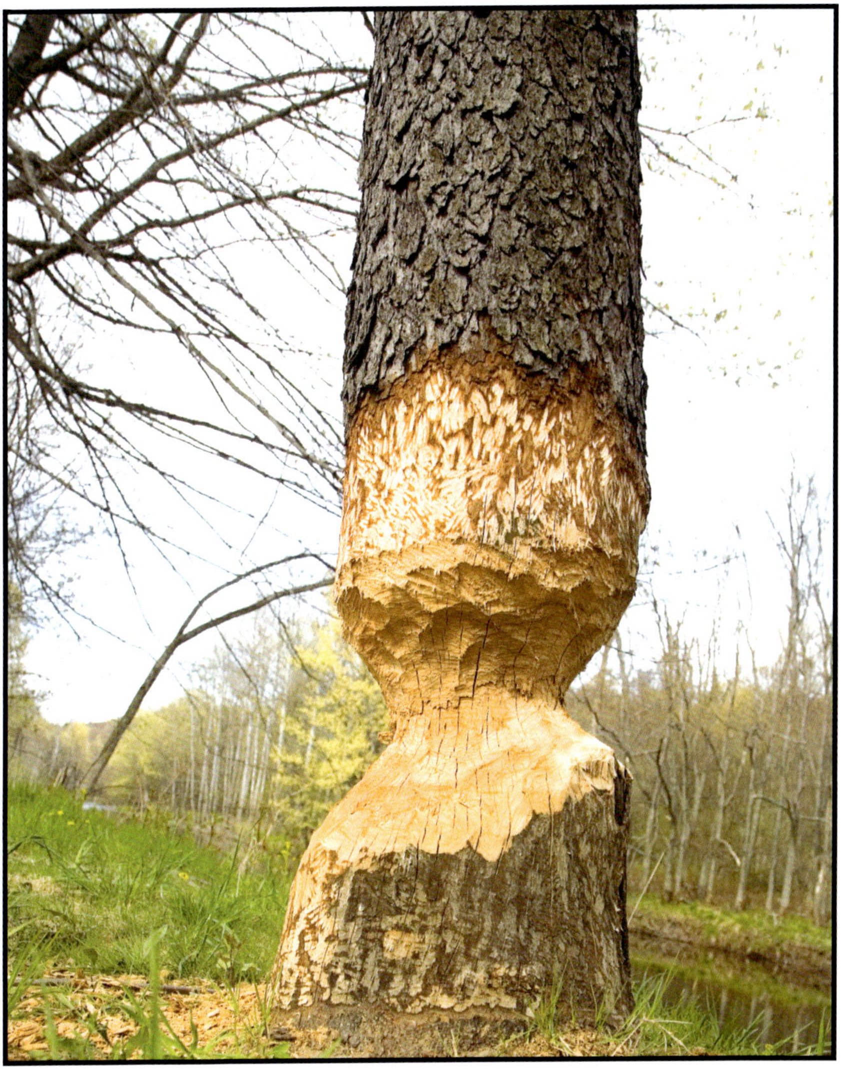

Beavers use wood.

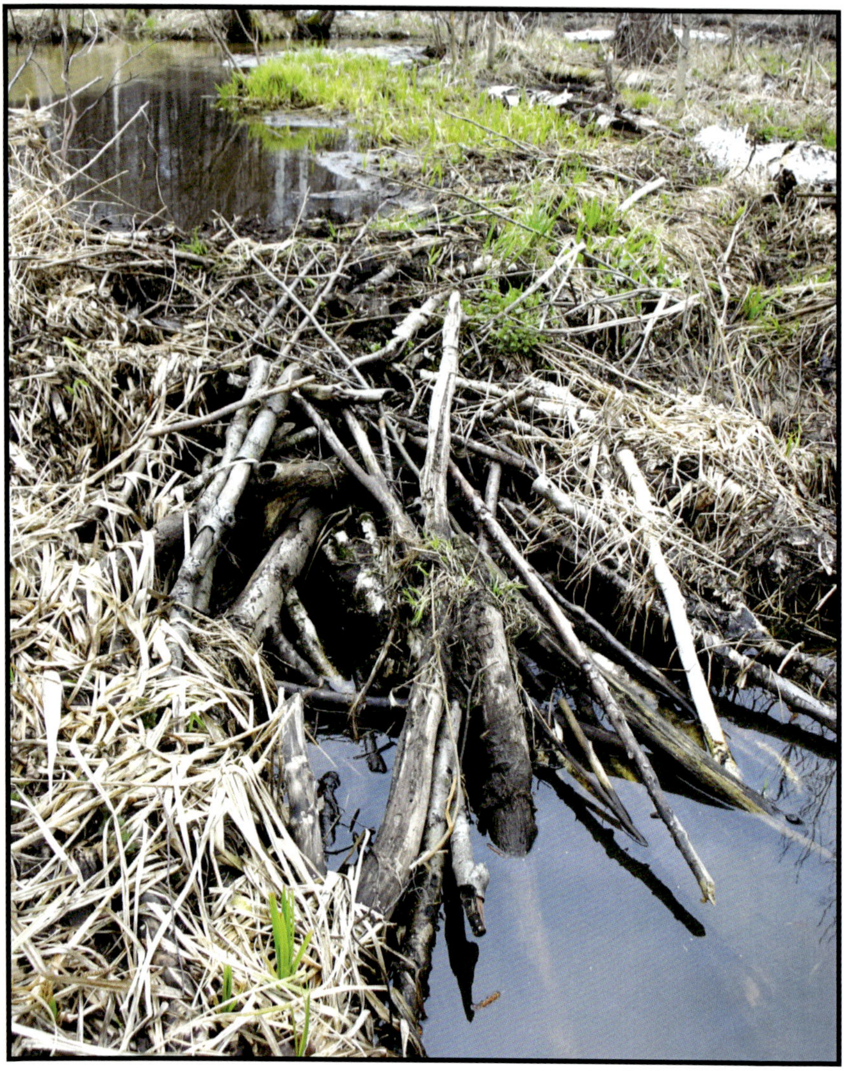

Beavers build dams.

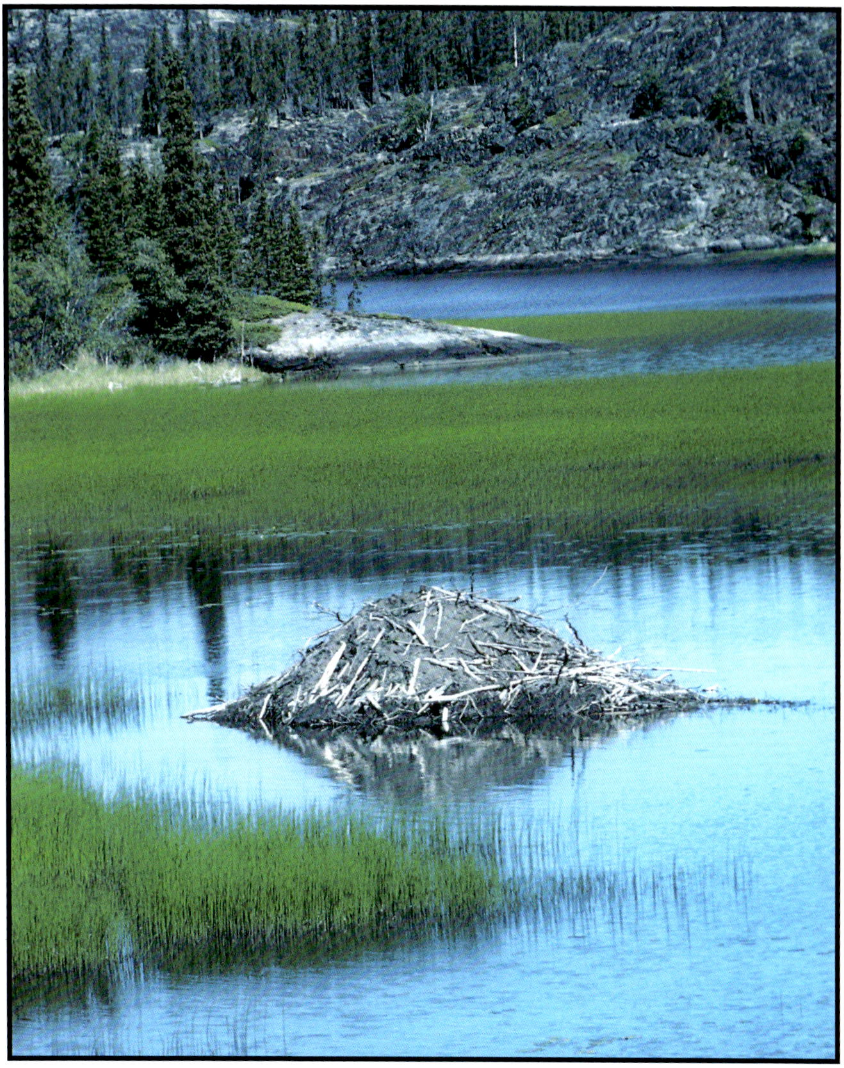

Beavers build homes.

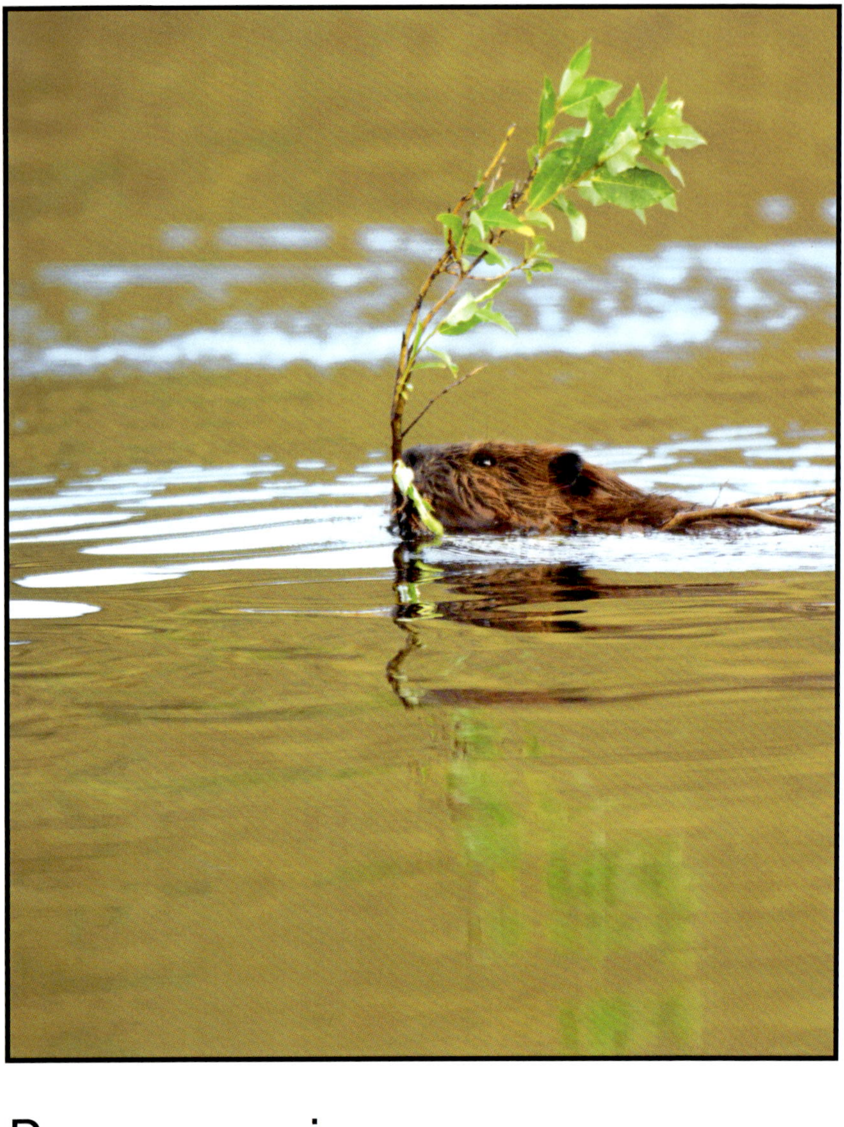

Beavers swim.

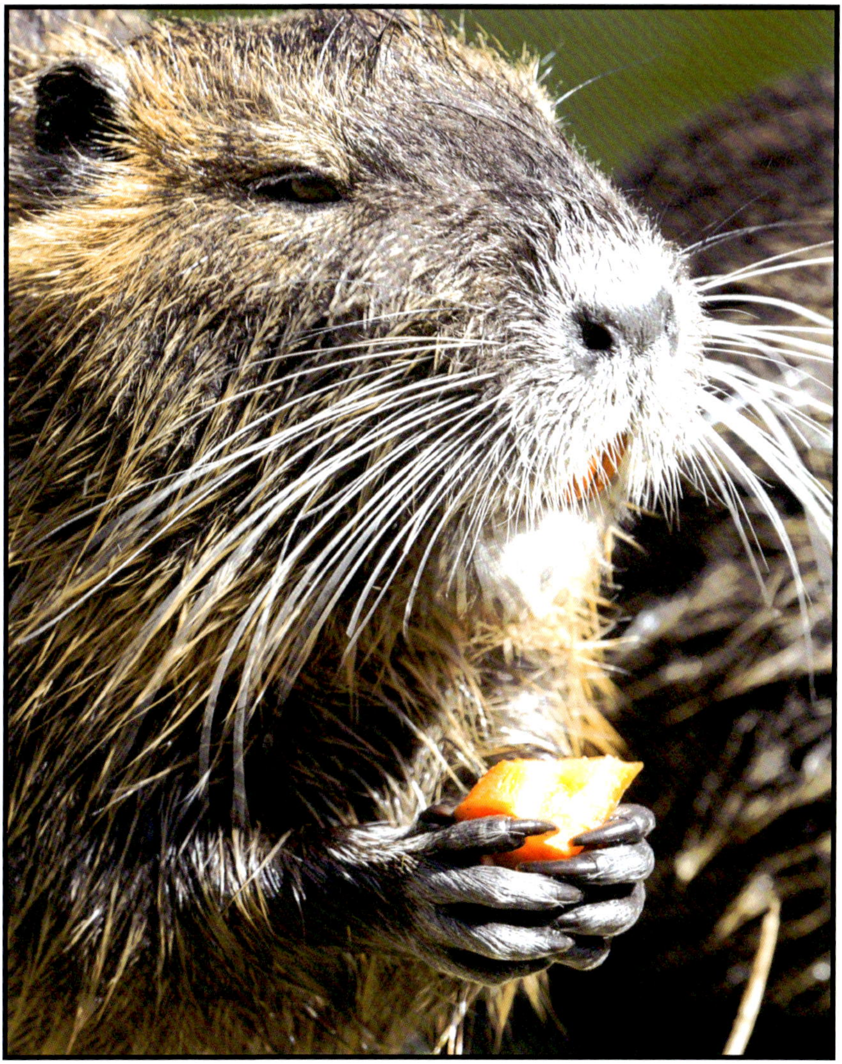

Beavers find food.

Words To Know

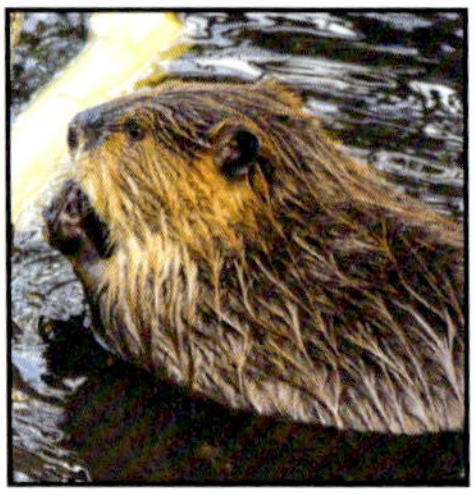

beaver

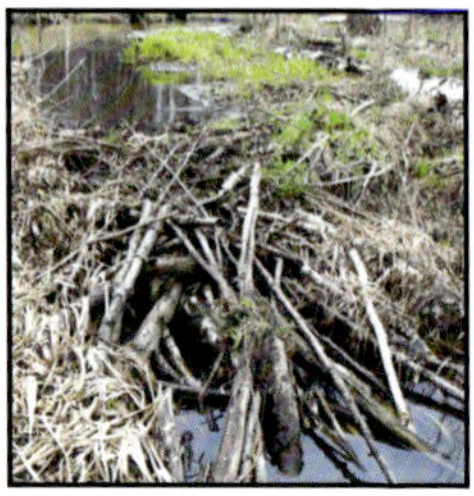

dam

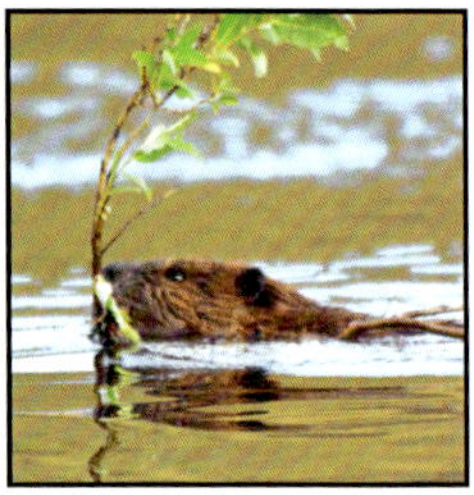

swim

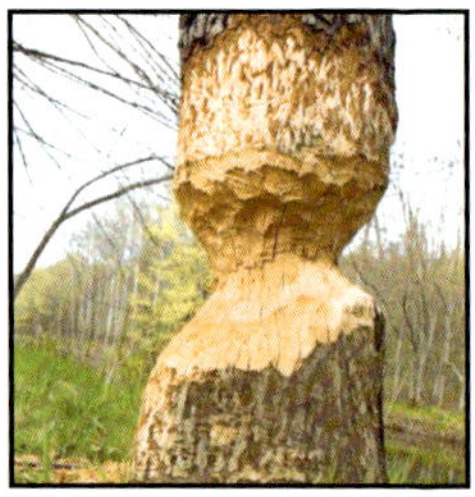

wood